It is a Joy
to Learn

Book Four
Revised Edition

Christian Liberty Press
Arlington Heights, Illinois 60004

A publication of
Christian Liberty Press
502 West Euclid Avenue
Arlington Heights, Illinois 60004
www.christianlibertypress.com

IT IS A JOY TO LEARN
    1. Phonics–Juvenile literature
    2. Reading–Juvenile literature
Written by
    Florence M. Lindstrom
Copyediting by
    Belit M. Shewan
    Edward J. Shewan
Cover Design by
    Eric D. Bristley

Illustrations by
    Vic Lockman
Colorization of Illustrations by
    Christopher D. Kou
Graphics and layout by
    Eric D. Bristley
    Christopher D. Kou
    Edward J. Shewan

ISBN 1-930092-30-X

Printed in the United States of America

Contents

Lesson 1

ou

cow house

Practice sounding these words, listening for the **ou** sound. Say them until you know them.

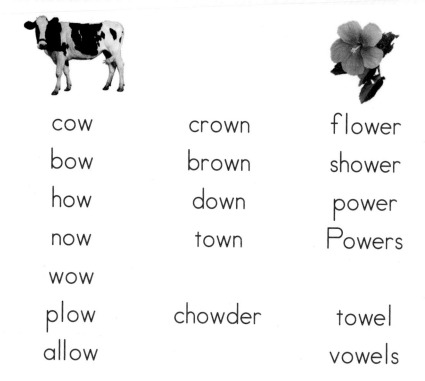

cow	crown	flower
bow	brown	shower
how	down	power
now	town	Powers
wow		
plow	chowder	towel
allow		vowels

Can you see Ted's brown cow?
A queen has a crown and a gown.
The vowels are a, e, i, o, and u.
Dad will allow me to go to town.
How are you now, brown cow?

Ted's Cow

Ted Powers has a big brown cow. He sat down to see how his cow will bow to eat the green grass.

Ted has flowers in his hand. Will he allow the cow to eat them? Yes, he will allow the cow to eat the flowers. They taste sweet to eat.

Wow, he can feel a rain shower! He will need to get a towel. He will now run home to get a towel.

His mother will give him chowder and milk for lunch. Ted will bow and thank God for blessing him.

Lesson 2

ou   cow house

Practice sounding these words, listening for the **ou** sound. Say them until you know them.

round	mouth	house
pound	south	mouse
sound		blouse
ground	shout	
found	out	
around	pout	loud
bound	about	proud

Jan will not pound on the piano.
Do not pout or shout in the house.
We must not jump on the couch.
Jan sings tunes with her mouth.
She sings about God's love.

Jan Plays the Piano

Jan is in the house. She has played with her dolls, but now she must play the piano. The sound is not loud, for she will not pound on the piano keys.

Dad can hear her sing with her mouth. She will not shout out loud. He likes to sit on the couch and hear her sing and play. He is proud of her.

She likes to sing tunes about God and His power and love. God is wonderful. He made Jan to be able to sing and play the piano.

Lesson 3

ou   cow house

Practice sounding these words, listening for the **ou** sound. Say them until you know them.

shower	scout	mountain
flower	sprout	fountain
power	out	
tower	about	
	shout	vacation
allow		interesting

It is interesting to see a mountain.
Tim found seeds on the ground.
Will the seeds sprout?
Yes, God makes seeds to sprout.
Will it rain when we take a vacation?

The Sprout

Tim and his family went to the mountains on a vacation. He likes to look or scout for interesting things to see. He found seeds on the ground. His father did allow him to take the seeds home.

Tim put one of the seeds down in a can. A shower of rain fell in the can. Now the seed is a sprout. It grew out of the can. The sprout will be a flower.

He will take the sprout into the house and tell his family about it. God made the seed to sprout.

Lesson 4

ou and ōw  cow bow

Practice sounding these words, listening for the two sounds of **ow**. Say them until you know them.

bōw	mōwer	windōw
grow		
mow	shower	our
show	power	flour
row	tower	
snow		out
know	warm	outside

Grandma sees out of the window.
An egg is found on the ground.
The children show Grandma.
It may hatch, if it is warm.
Our power mower cuts the grass.

6

An Egg in the Grass

Grandma can hear shouts outside the window. The children had found a tan egg on the ground near the house! They will show it to her.

May we take the egg to our house? Will it hatch? Will it grow?

You may take it if your mother will say yes. Do you know that you must keep it safe and warm? It may hatch and be a duck. Pick it up so the power mower will not hit it.

The egg did hatch into a cute duck. It always got out of its brown box. It now has a home outside of town.

Lesson 5

är   cart

Practice sounding these words, listening for the **är** sound. Say them until you know them.

cärd	cär	ärk
yard	bar	dark
hard	far	park
	jar	mark
	star	shark

large (j)

charge   marvelous   arm

Mark and Martha are in the car.
The children are in the backyard.
The park has a large swing set.
God made us in a marvelous way.
He gave us arms to help us.

The Children Play

The children are in the backyard. It is like a park. The day is not dark, so they cannot see the stars.

The children did work hard. They did help Mother with part of the work. Now they may go out in the yard to play with Martha. Mother is not far away.

They have a large slide. Mark stands at the top. Martha comes down on the slide. Their arms help them play. God has made them in a marvelous way. Can you hear the glad sounds they make?

är   cart

Practice sounding these words, listening for the **är** sound. Say them until you know them.

cärt	härp	ärm
art	sharp	harm
dart	carp	farm
part		
start	large (j)	Park
chart	charge	market
smart		carton

Ken has a carton with sharp tools.
He will start Miss Park's car.
He will charge the spark plugs.
She can now go to the market.
She will get new spark plugs too.

The Car

Miss Park has a large green car. She is going to the market to shop, but her car will not start.

Ken came with his tow truck to help her. He is smart and will do his part to start her car. He will charge the car so it will start.

He has a box of tools in his truck. Some of the tools are sharp and may harm us.

Ken tells Miss Park that her car needs new spark plugs. She pays him and thanks him for his help. Now she will go to the market.

Lesson 7

är   cart

Practice sounding these words, listening for the **är** sound. Say them until you know them.

ärk	yärn	ärch
bark	barn	march
mark		starch
park	card	
Sparkle	hard	garden
basket	away	alarm

Do you have a large pet cat?
Martha's cat is Sparkle.
It likes to run in the garden.
It may harm a dog if it barks.
Did you see the cat arch its back?

Martha's Cat

Martha has a large cat in her arms. The name of her cat is Sparkle. Martha will not harm her cat. She feeds it milk from a carton and gives it a basket for its naps.

Sparkle likes to go in the garden to see the bugs or catch a mouse. Sparkle will arch its back if it sees a dog. The dog may alarm Sparkle. The cat may harm the dog if it barks.

Sparkle likes to play with yarn. It will dart at the yarn. Martha is kind to Sparkle. Are you kind to your pet?

Lesson 8

är  cart

Practice sounding these words, listening for the **är** sound. Say them until you know them.

färming   yärn   ärm
farmed   barn   farm

                              harm
Carl   farm   alarm
              farmer

important   visit

Farmer Martin has a large farm.
Cows give us milk in the barn.
Sheep help us get yarn.
Hens give us eggs to eat.
Carl knows a farm is important.

Farmer Martin

Carl hears the alarm and starts to get up. Today he will visit Farmer Martin. His father will take Carl in the car, for the farm is far away. He knows that farms are important.

Farmer Martin will tell Carl about the farm. Farmer Martin has a large barn for his cows. The cows give milk. He has hens that lay eggs. He will sell some of the eggs in the market. Carl will see sheep that give us yarn.

Farmer Martin works hard. He thanks God for his farm. Carl is glad to visit Farmer Martin and help him with his work.

ôr  horse

Practice sounding these words, listening for the **ôr** sound. Say them until you know them.

fort	corn	storm
forty	born	
	torn	Jordan
port	worn	
sort	thorns	Corky
short		
sport		orchard

A storm came to the fort.
Corky is Jordan's pet pup.
Corky was born forty days ago.
Have you seen an apple orchard?
Do you like to play a sport?

Jordan's Pup

Jordan has a little pup. He was born just forty days ago, so he is still short. His name is Corky.

Jordan takes him in his fort. It is such fun to play with him. They run around the trees in the orchard. Corky likes to bite the apples. Jordan keeps him out of the thorns.

When there is a storm, Corky makes sort of a cry and stays near Jordan. Jordan is good to him. He is thankful for his dear little pet.

Lesson 10

ôr

horse

Practice sounding these words, listening for the **ôr** sound. Say them until you know them.

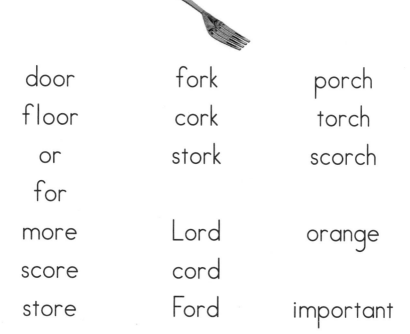

door	fork	porch
floor	cork	torch
or	stork	scorch
for		
more	Lord	orange
score	cord	
store	Ford	important

It is fun to play on the floor.
A happy family is important.
Will his score be more than mine?
Pick up your apple core.
Shut the door of the store.

A Happy Family

This family has been to the store but is now at home. As they sit on the floor, they like to play games and have fun. It is nice to work and play as a family. The Lord likes to see a family happy.

Will Father score more than the rest of them, or will he not win? He will be kind to them if he wins or not. I think he will be a kind sport.

It is time for Sam to move his orange marker. It is important that Sam will now score to win the game. Will Wag bark if Sam wins?

Lesson 11

ôr  horse

Practice sounding these words, listening for the **ôr** sound. Say them until you know them.

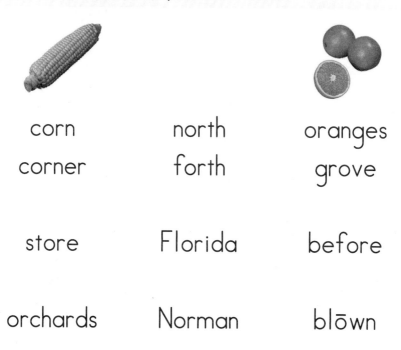

corn	north	oranges
corner	forth	grove
store	Florida	before
orchards	Norman	blōwn

Mr. Norman went to the store.
A big storm came from the north.
A grove is like an orchard or forest.
He ran to the corner of the block.
The oranges may grow in Florida.

The Storm

Mr. Norman is on his way home from work. A big wind storm has come from the north. Mr. Norman had his hat blown away. He must run fast, or it may get torn. I think Mr. Norman had to run to the corner of the block before he got his hat.

Mr. Norman will be happy to get home before it rains, but first he needs to stop at a store. He will get oranges that come from Florida. They grow in groves or orchards. It is hot in Florida, so the oranges grow large. Mr. Norman knows they are good for him to eat. Do you like to eat oranges?

Lesson 12

$\overline{oo}$

spoon

Practice sounding these words, listening for the $\overline{oo}$ sound. Say them until you know them.

spo͞on	sto͞ol	fo͞od
soon	cool	mood
noon	fool	
	pool	
	school	
balloon		goose
friend	birthday	choose

Martha's birthday is on Saturday.
Martha ate food with a spoon.
They will not have school.
Each friend may choose a balloon.
Do you want to choose a balloon?

Martha's Birthday

Today is a happy day. Martha is six years old. She is glad her friends came to her home. It is Saturday so they will not have school. They will not swim in a pool on this cool day.

At noon they ate some food with a spoon and now will have birthday cake. Soon they will play the game Duck-Duck-Goose. Do you see the balloons? Each friend may choose a balloon to take home. Martha is glad God has blessed her for six years. She will try to obey Him all her life.

Lesson 13

oo

spoon

Practice sounding these words, listening for the o̅o̅ sound. Say them until you know them.

to̅o̅th	bo̅o̅t	bro̅o̅m
booth	toot	room
	root	loom
loose		
goose	food	hoop
	mood	loop
poodle		scoop

Tom is in a happy mood today.
Tom has boots for when it rains.
Do you have a loose tooth?
See the poodle jump in a hoop.
Will you clean up your room?

Tom's Family

Tom is playing in his room. He can hear the sound of a car's horn toot. It is his father's car. He has come home. Tom will run to the door. He and his mother like to meet his father.

As the family eats food, Tom likes to tell about his day. He tells his father about his loose tooth. He tells how his poodle can jump in a hoop. He tells that his mother got him boots. His father smiles as he hears him speak. Tom likes to be with his father and mother. He is in such a happy mood. God has blessed little Tom with a wonderful family.

Lesson 14

$\overline{oo}$

spoon

Practice sounding these words, listening for the $\overline{oo}$ sound. Say them until you know them.

t$\overline{oo}$th	sp$\overline{oo}$l	br$\overline{oo}$m
booth	tool	room
	stool	loom
loose	school	boom
choose	pool	
		good
church	serve	
	telephone	people

We use tools to make a booth.
The booth is a little room.
It is a room for the telephone.
Bob and his father help at church.
It is a good way to serve the Lord.

Father Helps Bob

Bob and his father have work to do. They need to make a booth for church. It is hard work to make a good booth. It must not be loose. They will choose tools such as a hammer and nails for the work. Bob is glad as he helps his father.

The booth will be a little room for a telephone at church. It will help the people to hear as they speak. Bob and his father like to work and help at church. This is a good way to serve the Lord. Soon the booth will be made. At noon they will stop to eat some food.

Lesson 15

ŏŏ   book

Practice sounding these words, listening for the **ŏŏ** sound. Say them until you know them.

bŏŏk	push (ŏŏ)	wŏŏd
took	bush	good
look		stood
brook	pull	
	full	should
Bible		would
stories	put	could

The Bible is the best book.
It is full of stories and lessons.
We should read from it each day.
We could not read it in one day.
Look for good books to read.

The Best Book

Sam took a good book from his shelf. It is his Bible. It is the best book for him to look at and read. His sister will read it with him. Each day they should read part of the Bible.

The Bible tells us about God and what we should know and do. It tells us that we should love God and obey Him. It is full of true stories and lessons we should know. Sam and Jan could not read the Bible in a day. It is too big.

Soon he will put the book on his shelf. Then they will go out to play.

Lesson 16

oŏ

book

Practice sounding these words, listening for the oŏ sound. Say them until you know them.

foŏt	woŏd	boŏk
football	woods	toŏk
	woodpile	look
pull		cook
bush	would	brook
	could	
put	should	creature

Don is near a brook in the woods.
He put his foot in the brook.
He took a toad from the brook.
He would keep it if he could.
God made each creature we see.

A Toad From the Woods

Don has been in the woods. He found a toad in the brook near a bush. He put his foot in the brook to get it. He took the toad home so his mother could see it. Is she happy to look at it as she cooks?

His mother would not be happy if it should get into the bowl. Don asks if he could keep the toad. His mother tells Don that it is best to put the toad back in the brook near the bush in the woods. He will obey her.

God made each creature we see. Best of all He made you and me.

Lesson 17

ŏŏ

book

Practice sounding these words, listening for the ŏŏ sound. Say them until you know them.

wŏŏd		push (ŏŏ)
woods	cŏŏk	bush
good	look	
stood	brook	would
hood	hook	could
woodpecker	took	should
	book	

Dave's family has a good time.
A woodpecker lives in the woods.
The brook feels cool to Dave's foot.
Soon they will look in the woods.
Cookies should taste good.

The Woods

Dave's family has come for a picnic in the woods. They took a basket of food with them. Dave tells about a woodpecker he just saw in a tree.

Soon they will go and look around in the woods. Dave would like to put his foot in the cool brook. He should hold his father's hand, or he could slip. They will have a good time. The woods are full of wonderful things that God has made. First they will look for a spot to sit and eat the food and cookies that his mother has made. Would you like to go with them?

Lesson 18

oi   coin boy

Practice sounding these words, listening for the **oi** sound. Say them until you know them.

toys	moist	oil
toy	hoist	boil
boy		coil
joy	noise	soil
Roy		spoil
Joyce	voice	
enjoys		puppies

Joyce enjoys her pets.
Soil would spoil the rugs.
Moist means damp or wet.
The puppies know her voice.
I hope that you enjoy reading.

A Job for Joyce

Joyce has a big job. She must take care of her dog and its puppies. She enjoys them, but they make a lot of noise.

They got mud on their feet, so she had to give them a bath. She did not want them to get soil on the rug and spoil it. The dogs are still moist from the bath.

Joyce will find toys for them to enjoy. It is a joy to see them tug at the toys and run around as they play. She is kind to them. They run to her when they hear her voice.

Lesson 19

oi

coin boy

Practice sounding these words, listening for the **oi** sound. Say them until you know them.

boy	coin	moist
joy	join	hoist
toy	joint	
Roy	point	voice
enjoy		choice
joy	carrot	rejoice

The Lord blesses us with joy.
We enjoy playing in the snow.
Our suits get moist from the snow.
You have a choice of food.
We should not point at people.

The Snowman

Winter has come. These children enjoy playing in the snow. It is a good day to make a snowman, for the snow will pack.

Roy is a big boy and can hoist Jim up to put a nose on the snowman. The nose is orange and has a point. Do you know what the nose is? Yes, it is a carrot, which is a good choice for a snowman's nose.

It is a joy to hear the noise the children make with their voices as they enjoy playing. Soon they will come in and dry their moist suits.

Lesson 20

oi   coin boy

Practice sounding these words, listening for the **oi** sound. Say them until you know them.

toys	point	oil
joy	joint	boil
boy		foil
Troy	coin	soil
enjoy	join	spoil

Troy will not join the children.
He hears their happy voices.
He is a sick boy today.
He will enjoy his toys and books.
It is a joy to know God can heal.

A Sick Boy

Troy can see some children as they make a snowman. He can hear their voices make a happy noise. If he had a choice, he would join them.

Troy must stay inside and rest. He will be still. He is a sick boy. His mother will boil water for a hot drink that he will enjoy.

How glad he is that God will heal and make him well. He should not spoil the day by being sad. It is a time to enjoy playing with toys and reading books.

Lesson 21

û r

learn

Practice sounding these words, listening for the **û r** sound made by **ear**, **er**, **ir**, **ur**, and **(w)or**.

world	bird	earth
worship	girl	early
word	dirt	earn
worm	first	learn
work	sir	heard
worker	fir	pearl

God made this big earth.
He made each thing in this world.
We should love and obey the Lord.
Each person should try not to sin.
We will praise God for His works.

Our World

God made this world and all that is in it. It is a big earth and full of many things. God formed the large mountains and big lakes. He made the woods and each kind of bird, bug, and animal.

The first person He made was Adam. Adam's wife Eve was the first mother. They did not obey God, which made the world to be sinful.

In the Bible we read:

"Oh that men would praise the Lord for His wonderful works to the children of men." Psalm 107:8

Lesson 22

ûr   learn

Practice sounding these words, listening for the **ûr** sound made by **ear**, **er**, **ir**, **ur**, and **(w)or**.

circle	church	earth
circus	Kurt	early
third		learn
birthday	turn	heard
		jerk
grandfather	Saturday	corner
grandmother	Thursday	power

Saturday is a happy day for Kurt.
His grandfather comes to play.
They play with his birthday gift.
Grandfather gave him a train.
It runs in a circle if it has power.

Kurt's Pal

Kurt is so happy. It is Saturday, and his grandfather has come to play with him. He gave Kurt a train set for his birthday. His grandfather works on a train. Kurt's train will go in a circle when he turns on the power. He will learn to make it go so it will not jerk.

Kurt is so thankful for his dear grandfather and grandmother. He has heard about trips they have had in parts of the world. His grandmother made a sweater for him. He is glad they live just around the corner. They come to visit and go with him to church.

Lesson 23

ûr

learn

Practice sounding these words, listening for the **ûr** sound made by **ear**, **er**, **ir**, **ur**, and **(w)or**.

thirsty	nurse	sister
first	hurt	mother
girl	hurry	serve
third	curb	Fern
	sure (sh)	
Thursday	injured	worry
Saturday	disturb	button

Fern hurt her leg on a curb.
This is her first time in a hospital.
We must trust God and not worry.
Fern's sister and the nurse are kind.
We should not disturb a sick person.

Fern's Leg

Fern has hurt her leg. It was injured when she fell over the curb. This is the first time for her to be in the hospital. She will be a brave girl and not worry, for she is sure God will heal her leg.

Her sister has come to visit her. This will not disturb Fern, for her sister is a kind person. She will serve her some juice if she gets thirsty. If Fern needs help, she can push a red button and a nurse will hurry into her room. Fern came in on Thursday and will go home on Saturday.

Lesson 24

ûr

learn

Practice sounding these words, listening for the **ûr** sound made by **ear**, **er**, **ir**, **ur**, and **(w)or**.

worm	turtle	bird
worry	hurry	chirp
worth	turn	chirping
word	burn	dirt
work	disturb	
world	purple	early
worse	remember	heard

Have you heard a bird chirp?
A good child will not hurt a bird.
The birds find worms in the dirt.
God made birds to be interesting.
Remember to say "thank you."

Birds in the Nest

Early in the morning, Sam heard a chirping sound. He had to hurry out to take a look. He looked up to see a nest in the tree. Little birds were in the nest. A mother bird had a worm for her chicks to eat. Sam did not disturb or hurt them.

They need to eat lots of worms to help them grow. Birds must work hard to make the nest and feed the little birds. Do you know who made them to do this? Yes, it is God. Your father and mother work hard for you, too. Do you remember to thank them?

Lesson 25

ô

saw

Practice sounding these words, listening for the **ô** sound made by **o, al, au, aw, augh,** and **ough**.

dog	paw	ball
log	crawl	small
soft	straw	all
Softy	gnaw	
toss	lawn	saucer
song	Dawn	cause
strong	yawn	talk

Dawn will crawl on the lawn.
Her dog has a saucer of water.
Softy can yawn and sing a song.
Dawn will toss a ball to him.
He will not drink with a straw.

Dawn's Dog

Dawn likes to run on the lawn with her small dog Softy. He is a good dog and will not cause her to be sad. He can lift his paw for her. Dawn will get a saucer of cold water for him.

Softy can do lots of tricks. He can jump over a log. He can make his jaws go up and down so it looks like he can sing a song. His teeth are strong, and he likes to gnaw on a bone. He can catch a ball if Dawn will toss it to him. He can yawn, but he cannot talk or drink water with a straw. Dawn is glad that God made dogs.

Lesson 26

ô

saw

Practice sounding these words, listening for the **ô** sound made by **o**, **al**, **au**, **aw**, **augh**, and **ough**.

bought	law	song
brought	lawn	long
ought		belongs
thought	taught	wrong
fought	caught	
	naughty	Paul
money (ŭ)	daughter	Saul

Paul has bought a yellow bicycle.
He brought his bike home.
Dad saw it and thought it was nice.
Paul is glad it belongs to him.
God's law says it is wrong to steal.

Paul's Bicycle

Paul has bought a new yellow bicycle. He brought it home and is asking his father what he thought about it. Paul has worked hard with his job of mowing lawns. He has saved his money for a long time. He is so glad that this bicycle belongs to him now. He will try to take good care of it and obey the biking laws.

His father has taught him how he should give some of his money for the Lord's work. Paul thought he ought to do this. It would be wrong if he had kept it all for himself.

Lesson 27

ô  saw

Practice sounding these words, listening for the **ô** sound made by **o**, **al**, **au**, **aw**, **augh**, and **ough**.

bought	daughter	walk
thought	caught	talk
brought	taught	chalk
ought	naughty	stalk
baby	ball	cause
	mall	because

Mrs. Long has a dear daughter.
She ought not to crawl in the mall.
Is a naughty child happy?
They cause their parents to be sad.
We obey because we love them.

A Time to Shop

Mrs. Long is going to shop at the mall. She will fix the car seat so her small daughter will not fall as she drives. What do you think she tells her baby as she talks to her? Her baby is not naughty. When they get to the mall, Mrs. Long will hold her daughter as she walks.

Mothers and fathers are so happy if their children are not naughty or cause them to be sad or mad. All children should obey their parents in the Lord, because this is right (Ephesians 6:1). Will you try to be the kind and loving son or daughter that you ought to be?

Lesson 28

ô  saw

Practice sounding these words, listening for the **ô** sound made by **o**, **al**, **au**, **aw**, **augh**, and **ough**.

auto	moth	ball
	cloth	tall
long		fall
strong	off	small
wrong		
belong	branch	lawn
along	gone	crawl

toss   moss   boss   loss   gloss

Don's father bought a tire for his auto.
Dad used a long, strong rope.
Don thinks his father is thoughtful.
Don saw a frog, moth, and worm.

Don's Swing

How do you like to go up in a swing? Don thinks it is lots of fun. His father had gone to an auto shop and bought a new tire for his car. He used the old tire to make a swing on this tall tree. He had to toss a long, strong rope over the branch and tie a tight knot, so Don would not fall on the lawn and get hurt. Don trusts him and thanked him for being so thoughtful.

Don likes to be outside and see all the interesting things God made. Once he saw a frog hop off a log, a moth land on the soft moss, and a small worm crawl on the lawn.

Lesson 29

âr  stairs

Practice sounding these words, listening for the **âr** sound made by **air**, **are**, **arr**, **ear**, **eir**, **er**, **ere**, and **err**.

pair	parrot	bear
hair	carrot	pear
stair	carry	wear

square	cherry	where
care	very	there
share	errand	their

Grandmother sits in a chair and knits.
Larry will share a pear with her.
He will go there on an errand.
Where is your pair of shoes?

56

Larry Cares

Do you see that dear lady with the gray hair sitting on a chair? It is Larry's grandmother. He has gone on an errand for her. She is wearing a pair of shoes, but cannot walk down the stairs. He will go here and there where she asks him to go. He is very kind to her because he loves her. She loves Larry and trusts him to help her.

Soon Larry will come back with two pears to share with her. She asked him to carry a basket of yarn to her. She will share a story with Larry as she knits with the yarn. It is so dear to see their love and care for each other.

Lesson 30

ĕă

bread

Practice sounding these words, listening for the
short vowel **e** sound made by the vowel digraph **ea**.

feather	thread	sweater
weather	head	meant
leather	read	
Heather		wealth
breath	bedspread	health

ready	breakfast	instead

Heather meant to be ready.
She played and read instead.
Her sweater is by her bedspread.
It is pleasant to take a fresh breath.
Did you eat a good breakfast?

Always Be Ready

The weather was beautiful on this Sunday morning. The family had their breakfast and were in good health, so they were getting ready to go to Sunday School and church.

"Where is my red sweater, Mother?" asked Heather. "I cannot find my leather shoes. I meant to get my clothes ready last night. I played and read instead."

"Our morning would be much more pleasant if you got ready last night. Catch your breath and think. We want to please God in everything we do. Do I see something red by your bedspread?"